JESUS

...ers, please
latest
...

www.realreads.co.uk

Retold by Alan Moore and Gill Tavner
Illustrated by Karen Donnelly

Published by Real Reads Ltd
Stroud, Gloucestershire, UK
www.realreads.co.uk

ISBN 978-1-906230-24-1

Printed in China by Imago Ltd
Designed by Lucy Guenot
Typeset by Bookcraft Ltd, Stroud, Gloucestershire

CONTENTS

THE CHARACTERS

Jesus

As the Son of God, Jesus has been given an enormous task. What will this mean for him?

Mary and Joseph

They know that their son Jesus is special. How can they ensure that his childhood will prepare him for his future?

John the Baptist

Living in the wilderness, John's job is to prepare people for Jesus. How will he be rewarded for his work?

Mary Magdalene

When Jesus heals Mary, does he already know the role she will play in his work and in his life?

Simon Peter

Simon is a simple fisherman. What qualities does Jesus see in him? Will he let Jesus down or fulfil his hopes? Or both?

Judas

One of Jesus's twelve most trusted friends, what role will Judas play in his master's life?

Pharisees

Pharisees are men of God and men of the law. Why might they see Jesus as a threat? Will they listen to him?

5

JESUS OF NAZARETH

It wasn't until I went to see John the Baptist that I fully understood what my work was to be.

My childhood in Nazareth had been a happy one. I had friends, loving brothers and sisters and, of course, my mother and Joseph. My parents told me wonderful tales about my earliest days; I listened, fascinated, as their experiences became part of my identity.

As I grew older, Joseph taught me his trade. 'You'll need to earn a living one day,' he insisted.

Mary and Joseph were good Jews, observing the holy practices and teaching me the scriptures. The more I studied, the more these became my passion. 'I *need* to study and pray,' I tried to explain to my mother. 'I feel that I have an important job to do, even more important than Joseph's work.'

Mary looked concerned, but not surprised.

As I matured, my sense of purpose increased and my thoughts became more focused. All around me, people were making others' lives difficult. Those in greatest need of kindness, the sick and the poor, were often treated most cruelly. Some religious leaders created even more suffering by focusing on the law at the expense of compassion, or by exacting money from the poor. Surely this wasn't God's plan. Surely somebody needed to address these injustices.

I was still living at home when, just before my thirtieth birthday, a relative called Elizabeth visited us. She was concerned about her son. 'People call him John the Baptist,' she smiled. 'He's living rough in the wilderness south of Galilee, washing and baptising people in the River Jordan.'

We Jews were accustomed to ritual cleansing, but John was also urging people to change the way they lived, just as the prophets of long ago had taught. 'He claims to be preparing the way for somebody greater than him,' Elizabeth continued, 'somebody who will baptise us with the Holy Spirit and with fire.'

I remember the way my mother looked at me then. I saw sadness in her eyes as she whispered, 'You should visit him.'

Feeling a strong desire to be cleansed and present myself anew to God, I decided to walk the dusty miles to the verdant banks of the Jordan, where I found John.

'I've come to be baptised,' I said.

'I've been expecting you,' he greeted me, 'but surely it is *you* who should be baptising *me*.' I wondered what he meant.

As John submerged me in the cold river, I felt unexpected warmth in my heart. I suddenly saw all creation overflowing with God's love, and my heart was filled with a desperate love for everything.

As I burst joyfully out of the water,
the heavens opened to me,
and I heard a voice thunder,
'You are my son, with
whom I am well
pleased!'

I knew then for certain that I was the man
for whom John had been preparing the people. I
was God's son. This was the role for which I had
spent my life preparing.

My joy was soon replaced by fear and doubt.
The Son of God? What could that possibly
mean? What responsibilities did it carry?

Sons usually continued their father's work. As Joseph's son, I had continued his trade. My task now was to do God's work on earth.

Needing solitude, I walked away from the river and into the desert. I stayed in that barren place for many weeks, praying for guidance, asking God what he wanted me to do.

I had come without any food, and soon grew hungry. An evil voice, which seemed to come from outside my own self, suggested that as the Son of God I had enough power to turn the stones around me into food.

'Go on – try it,' urged the voice.

Though I was tempted, I knew this would be the wrong use of my power. I needed to pray, not think about food. I stopped worrying about my stomach, and it stopped nagging me.

So how *did* God want me to use my power? What *was* I capable of doing?

The hissing voice returned. 'Hey, Son of God, throw yourself from this cliff. You'll be fine – God will save you.'

'I already trust God. I don't need to test him.'

'Then show the people how powerful God is,' insisted the voice. 'Be a king, rule in his name.'

'No!' I shouted. 'No! People cannot be forced to love God!' The hissing voice was silenced.

There was only one way to do God's work. I had to give up everything. Modestly, selflessly and tirelessly, I had to show people how to love God, and how to treat each other. Whatever it might take, I had to make it possible for them to know – and to reach – God. Although I was afraid of where this might lead me, I knew that God would guide me.

I had been given a simple but enormous task. Leaving the desert, I walked for days towards the Sea of Galilee. Looking around me, I was pained more than ever by cruelty, injustice and greed. People thought that wealth was a blessing from God and, afraid of poverty, they clung to their possessions rather than sharing.

It wasn't only the poor who suffered. The sick were shunned, cast out from their villages and their families. People were afraid of sickness – they believed it was a punishment for sin.

In one town I saw the familiar sight of a lame beggar lying in the dust, his flesh covered with sores. Although he was begging for food, everybody walked straight past him. I had to act.

I challenged the passers-by. 'Aren't you ashamed to ignore this man's suffering?'

One man glanced in my direction. 'Please give him some food,' I pleaded.

The man hesitated, yet knelt with me beside the beggar. Touching the lame man, I felt God's power pass through me. 'Your sins are forgiven,' I breathed. I knew that God had given me the authority to forgive sin, but it must have been a strange thing to hear.

Trembling, the beggar stood up, his eyes widening as his sores healed. I too was trembling. Both men stared at me.

'How can you forgive sins?' marvelled the healed beggar. 'Only God can do that.'

Ignoring the question, I turned to the other man. 'Feed him as you would want to be fed if you were hungry.'

'Yes,' he replied, clearly moved. 'I will.'

God had granted me his love and courage to transform lives, and to bring people back to him. I continued to travel around Galilee, healing people and pleading with them to love each other.

Although my message was simple, many struggled to understand. As word spread about my work, the crowds grew larger. There were so many people with so many needs – I couldn't do this alone. 'Father,' I prayed, 'please send me the help I need.'

Early one evening I arrived on the Bethsaida shore of Galilee, where I noticed two fishermen casting their nets into the sea. I called out to them. They immediately drew in their nets and hurried towards me. They were brothers, Andrew and Simon.

We ate together, and as we talked I realised that God had answered my prayer. 'Come with me,' I said, 'and I will make you fishers of people.'

After a brief pause first Simon, then Andrew, stood up and followed me along the shore. We met two more fishermen brothers, James and John. I knew that God wanted them to help me too. They were working with their father at the time, but without hesitation they left him and followed me.

The five of us walked into Capernaum, where Simon and Andrew welcomed us into their home. My friends, being plain, honest fishermen, were able to talk to the local people in a way that was easily understood. God had chosen well.

God needed me to speak wherever people gathered, so I visited synagogues and taught from the scriptures. One such afternoon, a man burst into the synagogue. 'What do you want, Jesus of Nazareth?' he shrieked. 'Have you come to destroy us?'

I heard people around me murmur that he was possessed by an evil spirit. I placed my hand on the man. 'Come out of him!' I commanded the spirit. The poor man fell screaming to the floor, and then was perfectly calm.

'Who are you?' somebody asked in awe. 'Even evil spirits obey you.'

In the early days it was easy to find the peace and quiet I needed to pray, to gather my strength, and to think ahead. But news travels faster than human feet, and soon I could no longer enter a village without a crowd surrounding me. Sometimes I yearned to escape, and my friends tried to protect me, but still the people flocked.

I saw in their faces that their need for compassion was far greater than my need for rest. Some were despairing, some angry. Many were lost. I knew what it was to be human, to feel lost and afraid. How could I turn anybody away? Can any shepherd turn his back on a lost lamb?

In spite of their poverty, people provided us with food and shelter. In one village God sent me Mary Magdalene, a woman who was deeply troubled and desperately wanted to be healed.

With God's help I was able to heal her, and from then on Mary supported our work. She had money of her own, which she gladly offered to help us to be more effective in God's service.

Teachers of Jewish law often visited us at Simon's house, which had become our base.

One such afternoon I was explaining the nature of forgiveness. 'Surely only God can forgive sins,' one teacher fretted.

Outside, we could hear the familiar sounds of a crowd gathering. We tried to continue our discussion, but after a while were distracted by sounds above us. Simon leapt to his feet. 'They're breaking through my roof!' he cried. It was true – we looked up and saw daylight.

When the hole was large enough, a sleeping mat, suspended on ropes, was slowly lowered. On the mat lay a man. 'He is paralysed, Rabbi,' a voice called from the roof.

'But we know that you can heal him.'

I felt their faith move within me as I knelt beside the man and took his hand. 'Your sins are forgiven,' I said quietly.

Some of the teachers gasped. I sensed their disapproval even before they spoke. Who was I, a mere man, to forgive people's sins? Saddened by their inflexibility and lack of compassion, I turned to the paralysed man. 'Take up your mat and go home.'

Amazed, the man tested the strength of his legs. Standing tentatively, he rolled up his mat and thanked me. His friends on the roof cheered.

Some of the teachers were perturbed. Having spent their lives studying and rigidly applying the laws given by Moses, it was difficult for them to understand the true nature of God's love. I wished they could understand that people must forgive each other, just as God will always find a way to forgive us.

Whenever I healed someone I was accused of blasphemy against God. It seemed so hard to show people that God's law is about love and forgiveness. What would it take?

I found myself in unwelcome conflict over another issue too.

Jewish law states that the Sabbath must be a holy day, free from work. It's a sensible law, guaranteeing us space in each week to think about what God wants of us, rather than concentrating on the day-to-day concerns of our lives. Unfortunately, though, many teachers placed too much emphasis on the Sabbath's restrictions and rules, rather than on its opportunities for rest and reflection.

One Sabbath, as I entered the synagogue, I saw a man with a withered hand. A tense silence descended. People watched intently, waiting to see whether I would heal him on the Sabbath.

'Stand up,' I urged the nervous man. Then I turned to the people. 'Which is lawful on the Sabbath,' I asked them, 'to do good or to do evil?'

Nobody said a word.

Here was an opportunity for me to demonstrate both God's compassion and his authority.

I turned back to the man. 'Stretch out your hand.'

As he held out his trembling hand, it began to grow and fill. He moved it around. He clenched and unclenched his fist. Most people gasped, but some remained stony-faced. I knew then that there were people who would try to stop my work. Most people, however, wanted to be guided towards living a good life. They wanted to be pure before God.

The crowds following me continued to grow. Sometimes it was difficult to address so many people. I often stood on higher ground to talk, so that more might see and hear.

When teaching by the lakeside, I used to take a boat onto the water and speak from there.

How could I reach more people? I realised that I needed to choose some special people from amongst my closest followers, people who could help me spread the message.

I chose twelve. In Simon the fisherman I saw a man who, in spite of his mistakes – perhaps because of them – could be a rock on which I could build the future. I called him Peter, meaning 'rock'. I also chose his brother Andrew.

I nicknamed James and John 'the sons of thunder' because of their powerful preaching.

The others I chose were Philip, Bartholomew, Matthew, Thomas, James bar Alpheus, Thaddeus, another Simon, and Judas Iscariot. To Judas, an educated, conscientious man, I gave responsibility for the group's money.

Before these men could teach and heal, they still had much to learn. I had to prepare them. 'Tell people stories, or parables,' I advised them. 'If we simply repeat the laws, they'll follow them rigidly. Parables help people to apply God's law to their lives. We have to help them to understand God's message in a way that makes sense to them.'

I explained how important it was for the twelve to set a good example. 'Be generous; don't hide the light of God's love. If you show love and compassion, others will learn from you. Like seed sown on good soil, the word of God, sown by you, will produce a crop a hundred times what was sown. The seeds will grow and multiply without you having to do any more work. This is what God's kingdom is like. We must create the kingdom of God on earth.'

I faced a difficult dilemma. I needed to reach as many people as possible, but I was reluctant to draw attention to myself. The Romans ruled our country with a reasonably gentle hand, often cooperating with the Jewish authorities. I didn't want to threaten them. I wasn't seeking conflict.

Though I frequently asked people not to talk too much about the things we did, people gathered in large groups to hear what we had to say, and people needing help continued to seek us out. Having crossed the lake one day, I was greeted on the shore by another crowd, led by Jairus, a synagogue elder. He was deeply distressed.

'My daughter is dying,' he wept. 'Please heal her.'

As I followed Jairus through the crowd, I suddenly felt a familiar healing flow of love. I stopped and looked round. 'Who touched the fringe of my robe?' I asked. It must have seemed a strange question in the midst of a jostling crowd.

A woman edged forward. 'I'm so sorry,' her voice trembled, 'it was me. I've been ill for years and no doctor has been able to help me.'

'Daughter, your faith has healed you,' I said. 'Go in peace.'

As we approached Jairus' house, two men ran out. 'Jairus, we're so sorry. She is dead!'

'Don't be afraid,' I reassured Jairus. 'Believe.'

Jairus led me to where his daughter lay. Taking her hand, I spoke to her gently. 'Talitha koum. Little lamb, arise.'

The child opened her eyes, stood up, and walked over to her mother. I asked those within the house to tell nobody what had happened. With such a large, anxious crowd waiting outside, however, there was little chance of that.

I hadn't visited my family in Nazareth for almost two years. It was time to return.

My family welcomed me. That Sabbath, in the familiar synagogue, I read aloud from the scriptures. My former friends and neighbours listened in silence. A chill breeze of resentment whispered to me from the crowd, making me shiver. It warned of approaching storms.

Later, in the street, two men confronted me. 'Who do you think you are?' one of them challenged. 'You're just a craftsman, Mary's son!' More men gathered.

I was astonished by their hostility. I reminded myself that a prophet is never welcomed in his own town. Saddened, I walked through the angry crowd. Nobody tried to stop me.

More sadness was to follow. News reached us that John the Baptist had been beheaded under King Herod's orders. Herod was a God-fearing man, but he was weak. Although he had recognised John's virtue, he had feared his power and influence. He had surrendered to his fear. I grieved both for John and for Herod.

We were living in dangerous times, but God's work had to be done. My twelve friends were now ready for their important task. I sent them off in pairs so they could support each other. 'You are now my apostles, my disciples. You have God's authority to preach and to heal,' I told them. 'Take nothing with you; God will provide everything you need.'

Several weeks later the twelve returned, tired but elated. We tried to find a secluded place down by the shore so we could share our experiences without being disturbed by crowds of people, but it was impossible. The people, like lost sheep looking for their shepherd, followed us. I loved them, and could not ignore them. That evening, we fed all five thousand.

At nightfall I advised the apostles to take the boat out on the lake. I would join them later. When I eventually found them, a storm was blowing. Though their fear sometimes exposed weaknesses in their faith, I learned that they had done their work well.

The following morning we sailed across Galilee to Gennesaret, where we taught and healed for several days. While we were there, we were constantly and openly watched by a group of Pharisees, strict teachers of the law. They often came over to talk with us and challenge us.

One day we stopped to eat in the market. Hungry and tired, we were enjoying a brief respite from the crowds. My heart sank when I saw a group of frowning Pharisees approaching. One man, who had been particularly confrontational in previous conversations, cleared his throat. 'Ahem. Why didn't you carry out the ritual cleansing before you ate?'

I sighed. 'Nothing can make us impure just by going into our body,' I explained.

We were attracting attention, and a small group gathered round us. 'This food, coming from the outside, will pass through our stomachs and come out again.' Someone laughed. 'It is the things that come from the inside – our thoughts and feelings – which have the power to make us clean or unclean.'

I was beginning to understand that my work would not be complete until I had sacrificed my life, as was foretold in the scriptures. By sacrificing me, his own son, God would prove that there is nothing that can separate people from his love.

Seeking closeness to God, I took Simon Peter, James and John to a mountaintop to pray. I felt God's presence there more intensely than ever before – it reminded me of my baptism in the Jordan. As I prayed, I was enlightened with deeper understanding. Moses and Elijah appeared beside me and, as at my baptism, I heard God's voice saying 'This is my beloved son.'

Later, as we descended the mountain, I knew what I had to do.

Although my disciples were good men, their faith and understanding sometimes failed them. Sensing that my time on earth was limited, I occasionally felt frustrated by them, the kind of frustration a loving parent experiences towards their child. 'How much longer must I be with you?' I once asked. And, like children, they sometimes argued amongst themselves about who was the most important. 'The one who wants to be the greatest must learn to be the servant of all,' I reminded them.

In their concern to shield me from crowds, the disciples once tried to usher away a group of women who had brought their children to be blessed. I stopped them. 'Let the children come,' I said. 'The kingdom of God belongs to such as these.'

Unsophisticated, dependent, innocent, and willing to learn – that is how we should all be before God.

A little later a young man, clearly wealthy, approached me. 'Teacher,' he asked, 'what must I do to enter God's kingdom?'

I smiled. He genuinely wanted to do God's will but, as for so many people, an obstacle stood between him and God. His obstacle was his wealth. 'Sell everything you have and give it to the poor,' I advised him. 'Then follow me.'

The man's face fell. He couldn't do it. He turned dejectedly and walked away. That night I prayed for him.

As I explained to the disciples, 'It is impossible for the rich to enter the kingdom of Heaven. You must forsake everything.'

'We have forsaken everything,' said Simon Peter anxiously.

'And you shall have your reward,' I reassured him. I didn't tell him how much he would have to suffer before he received it.

Our journey was leading us relentlessly towards Jerusalem, towards confrontation. It was time to prepare my disciples for what lay ahead.

'In Jerusalem I will be betrayed to the chief priests.' They listened quietly. 'They will condemn me to death. People will mock, flog, and kill me. Three days later I will rise from the dead.' The men were pale and silent.

The time for quiet reasoning and diplomacy had run out. Did this mean I had failed? Many people had heard my message and believed, others were still trying. However, the religious and political authorities were making people's lives ever more difficult. Significant change now called for significant action.

I rode into Jerusalem on a colt, as predicted in the scriptures. A crowd followed. More crowds gathered along the way to welcome me, singing psalms of expectation. 'Hosanna in the highest!' they called, as they tore down palm

branches and laid them before my colt's feet.
The palm was a national emblem, a symbol of
Jewish unity. A threat.

'They welcome you as a king!' observed
Simon Peter. The disciples were excited. Some
of them had been longing for this action. They
thought we were finally challenging the right
of the Romans to rule over us; even that we
were challenging the Jewish authorities. But
the true purpose of what lay ahead was far
greater than any of them could imagine.

'Blessed is he who comes in the name of the Lord!' shouted the crowd. 'Blessed is the coming kingdom!'

Our work in Jerusalem had begun. I led the procession to the temple to pray but, dismayed by what I found there, I asked the crowd to disperse, and took the disciples out of Jerusalem. We would return tomorrow.

A temple is supposed to be a peaceful place, where people can hear God's voice. Instead of peace, however, we had encountered a cacophony of moneychangers and people selling animals for sacrifice. Traders were using the temple court as a short cut as they crossed the city, bartering as they went. In what was supposed to be a place of prayer and contemplation, God's voice was being drowned out by the din.

The following morning, at the entrance to the temple, I saw a tough-looking man trying to exact temple tax from a weeping woman. Furious, I overturned his table. The disciples followed my lead, turning over tables and benches, causing chaos.

I had to make people see what they were doing. From the top of the steps I called out, 'It is written, "my house will be called a house of prayer for all nations", but *you* have turned it into a den of thieves!'

The chief priests were angry and afraid. They knew we were right.

The next day we returned to the temple, where people were now praying peacefully. A group of priests and elders confronted us. 'What authority do you have to do these things?' they asked.

Of course, I had God's authority, but I was aware that they were looking for an opportunity to accuse me of blasphemy. I refused to answer.

Challenges like this became more frequent and more hostile. I recognised fear in the faces of my challengers, the fear that would lead to my death. They tried to trap me in their webs of words. How sad they made me feel. Sad and tired.

'Teacher, you are a man of integrity,' began one young man, keen to try his wit. 'Tell us, should we pay taxes to Caesar or not?'

I must have sighed, for he smiled, thinking he had scored a significant victory. If I answered that they should not pay taxes to Rome, I could be arrested for sedition. If I advised them to pay taxes, the oppressed would probably reject me and my ideas.

'Why are you trying to trap me?' I asked. 'Show me a denarius.' I held up the coin. 'Whose portrait is this?' We all knew that it was Caesar's, and that the inscription on the coin proclaimed him a god. As this broke one of our commandments, Roman coins were deeply offensive to Jews.

'Why, it is Caesar,' answered my young challenger.

'Then give to Caesar what is Caesar's, and give to God what is God's. God doesn't need our money, he needs our hearts.'

Not all questions were hostile. One Pharisee asked me, 'Which is the most important of the commandments?'

I could see that he was a good man. 'The most important commandment is this,' I replied, 'that you love God with all your heart, with all your soul, with all your mind, and with all your strength. The second is this: love your neighbour as yourself.'

My questioner smiled. 'Rabbi, you are right. To love God and to love each other is more important than anything else.'

I smiled. 'You are not far from the kingdom of God,' I told him.

Though we visited the temple daily, our base at the time was outside Jerusalem, in the village of Bethany. One evening we were relaxing after dinner when a woman entered the room, carrying a long-necked alabaster jar filled with expensive perfume. Breaking the neck of the jar, she poured some of the perfume over my head.

'What a waste!' exclaimed Judas.

'She should have sold the perfume and given the money to the poor.'

Poor Judas. After three years of being responsible for our money, his reaction was natural. 'She has done a beautiful thing,' I corrected him. 'The poor will always be with you. You can help them any time, but you will not always have me. She poured perfume over me to prepare me for my burial.'

The disciples shuffled uncomfortably.

It was Passover, the greatest celebration of the Jewish calendar. Some of the disciples went ahead into Jerusalem to find and prepare a room for our meal. Although I had tried to warn them of what lay ahead, they did not realise just how soon the real trouble would begin. This was to be the last meal we would share together.

After a rather sombre meal together, we reclined in silence at the table. Although the mood was melancholy, we were physically and spiritually very close. It was time for me to address a difficult issue. These poor men.

'My friends,' I began, 'very soon one of you will betray me.' I knew that the betrayal was already under way, and I knew who it was.

Disbelieving, the men sat up. The closeness we had been enjoying just seconds before was replaced by suspicion and fear. 'Surely it is not me!' some exclaimed. 'Who is it?'

'It is one who dips bread into the bowl with me.'

Judas, who was dipping his bread into my bowl at that moment, swiftly drew back his hand. I wondered if any of the others had noticed.

It was necessary for God's plan that somebody should betray me, but it was a dreadful responsibility to bear.

Judas looked ashen. From this moment on, his life would be unbearable. In the confusion that followed, Judas rose weakly from his seat and left the room.

There was still work to be done. Picking up a loaf of bread, I thanked God and broke it. Passing it around, I said quietly, 'Take this; this is my body.' It symbolised all that I was; all that we had shared. Their faces were desperately unhappy. Some wept.

I picked up the wine cup. Again I thanked God and passed it among the eleven remaining disciples. 'This is my blood, God's new promise, poured out for you and for all people.'

They understood how important this promise was, but still did not fully comprehend what I had to do.

That night I went to the Mount of Olives to pray. My friends loyally accompanied me, but again I had to tell them a painful truth. 'Tonight, when they come for me, you will all run away.' To stay by my side would mean almost certain death. They were only human, after all.

Simon Peter was hurt and adamant. 'I won't leave you,' he insisted.

He was right. I knew he would never leave me, but his courage would have a limit. 'Tonight, before the cockerel crows twice,' I told him sadly, 'you will disown me three times.'

Tonight, more than ever before, I needed to pray for strength to endure the suffering that lay ahead. We walked to the garden at Gethsemane, my favourite place on the Mount. Leaving most of the men near the entrance to the garden, I took Peter, James and John with me. 'Stay here and keep watch,' I told them.

Having walked a short distance away from them, I fell to the ground, overwhelmed with sorrow. 'Father, you can do anything. If it is your will, take this cup of suffering from me.' My prayer was not answered. I did not find peace.

Returning to my friends, I found them sleeping. I felt terribly alone. 'Couldn't you keep watch for just one hour? You must stay awake!' Again I went to pray, but when I returned they had gone to sleep again. My grief was immense. My prayers were still unanswered.

On my third attempt I finally found God's calming presence. He gave me courage and peace of mind, and reminded me that this was the work for which I had been born. I found my friends asleep yet again. Reluctantly, I woke them. When I looked up, I saw Judas approaching with a group of armed men.

'Here comes my betrayer,' I said quietly,

Smiling, but ashamed to meet my eye, Judas greeted me and identified me with a kiss. I longed to comfort him, but there was no time. The guards seized me roughly. I tried to explain to them what they were doing, but they wouldn't listen.

As they led me away I accepted that the scriptures must be fulfilled. My disciples were nowhere to be seen.

The chief priest called his council together. There was never any doubt what the outcome of my trial would be. I pitied those who gave false evidence against me. Eventually the chief priest challenged me directly. 'Are you the Son of God?'

'I am,' I replied. 'You will see me sitting at God's right hand.'

'You heard the blasphemy!' he cried in triumph. He tore his clothes, a sign that he was condemning me to death.

I spotted Simon Peter hiding in the shadows, watching. My poor friend. What fear, what pain he must be suffering. Later I heard a cockerel crow twice, but I knew Simon Peter would never desert me. When I was no longer there he would be my rock, my foundation.

Early next morning they presented me to Pontius Pilate, the Roman prefect of the province. I sensed his discomfort as he questioned me. 'Are you the King of the Jews?'

I knew he wanted me to deny that I was, so he could release me, but I couldn't help him.

A crowd had gathered outside Pilate's palace. I was accustomed to crowds, but this one was different. Although I recognised some people in the sea of faces, many more were strangers, relishing the mounting hysteria. Priests prowled amongst the people, whispering, preparing them for their roles in the unfolding drama.

Pilate saw only one way to avoid responsibility. He handed the decision to the crowd, publicly washing his hands of his own guilt. 'What shall I do with the King of the Jews?' he asked.

At first just a few voices called, 'Crucify him!', but it soon grew into a loud, steady chant. 'Crucify him! Crucify him!'

'Why? What crime has he committed?' asked Pilate in disbelief.

The crowd continued chanting, baying for blood.

I was to be flogged and crucified. Unbearable suffering lay ahead. The brutal flogging would tear my flesh from my bones. People had died from these floggings alone. Later, they would drive iron spikes through my wrists, nailing me to a wooden beam. They would fix the beam to an olive trunk, driving another spike through my ankles. The sun's heat would be unbearable. When my damaged limbs could no longer support my weight, I would suffocate.

Experiencing human suffering through me – his own son – God would show that his love and forgiveness have no limits. Though I was weak and exhausted, I had to carry the beam for my own cross to a nearby cliff called Golgotha, 'the place of the skull'.

When I struggled under the weight of my beam, soldiers pulled a man from the crowd to help me. At Golgotha, other soldiers drove in the spikes. The agony made it hard to breathe,

hard to think, but I found the words to forgive. Then I prayed, trusting that people would finally understand and could start afresh. It was only my flesh that they hurt.

My final hours were long. As the end of my suffering drew near, I remembered a song to God from our scriptures, a psalm of despair and hope.

My God, why have you forsaken me? You are the holy one, the praise of Israel. Our fathers trusted you and were delivered, but I am scorned and despised by the people. All who see me mock me, saying 'He trusted in the Lord; let the Lord rescue him.'

From birth I was cast upon you; from my mother's womb you have been my God.

Do not be far from me, for trouble is near and there is no one to help.

I am poured out like water and all my bones are out of joint, my heart is like melted wax.

My throat is as dry as dust and my tongue sticks to the roof of my mouth.

You lay me in the dust of death.

People stare and gloat over me.

They divide my garments among them, and cast lots for my clothing.

Lord, do not be far from me.

Then my human suffering ended, but I was still in the world. I still had to explain to my friends that my death had opened up a new way to God for everyone. Only when they understood this would I be free to ascend to my father in heaven.

TAKING THINGS FURTHER
The real read

This *Real Reads* volume of *Jesus of Nazareth* is our interpretation of the events of the New Testament, told from the perspective of its most important participant. In writing this account of Jesus's life, we have used evidence from the gospel according to Mark. This is one of the four gospels – the first four books of the New Testament.

It is important to acknowledge that all four gospels were written after Jesus's death, and that the writers had different aims in mind – although they all wanted to engender faith in the reader that Jesus was the Son of God. The first three gospels – Matthew, Mark and Luke – are called 'the synoptic gospels'. They were probably written between forty and sixty years after the crucifixion. The gospel according to John, written later, is significantly different.

Sometimes, the four gospels' accounts of events differ considerably. At first this made our task rather difficult, until we realised that what we needed to do was present the New Testament as it is, rather than to weave a path of our choice between the gospels. Therefore, if you read all six books in the *Real Reads* New Testament series, you may well notice some of the apparent contradictions and inconsistencies that are present in the Bible itself.

In writing each of the six *Real Reads* New Testament books we chose a specific source to follow. To write Jesus's account of his life and ministry we used Mark's gospel, because it is widely considered to be the earliest of the gospels. We felt it is therefore most likely to be the closest to Jesus's actual words. We also feel that it gives the most personal and moving version of Jesus's death.

Jesus did not write down his own experiences, so we do not know what he thought of the events through which he lived. Using thorough research and paying close attention to the Bible account, we have tried to imagine what he might have been like, and what he might have thought.

This *Real Reads Jesus of Nazareth* does not cover all the events of the New Testament. Reading the other five books in the series will bring you closer to an understanding of the complete story. You may then want to read the New Testament itself. We recommend that you read either the *New International Version* or *The Youth Bible*, details of which are given below.

Biblical sources

On the *Real Reads* website you will find an online concordance (www.realreads.co.uk/ newtestament/concordance/jesus). A 'bible concordance' is an indexing tool which allows you to see how the same words, sentences and passages appear in different versions and translations of the Bible. This online concordance will direct you from events in the *Real Reads* version back to their biblical sources, so you can see clearly where each part of our story is drawn from. Although *Jesus of Nazareth* is based on the story as told in the gospel of Mark, there are a few places where we have drawn on other sources.

Life in
New Testament times

The main events of Jesus's life took place in Palestine, a long narrow area of land bordered to the west by the Mediterranean Sea and to the east by the Transjordanian Desert. Some parts of Palestine were desert, some were hill country, some rich pasture land, and some uncultivated wilderness.

Although Palestine was Jewish land, it was part of the Roman Empire and under Roman control. The Jews resented paying taxes to Rome. During Jesus's lifetime, there was considerable conflict between the Jews and their Roman rulers. This helps to explain why the Romans might have been nervous of the crowds following Jesus.

The Jews considered Palestine to be their 'promised land', promised to them by God. Moses had led them there from slavery in Egypt. The area was mainly Jewish, with synagogues and temples. Nevertheless, it is interesting that most of Jesus's ministry took place around the Sea of Galilee, an area with a mixed population of Jews and Gentiles, and a reputation for political unrest.

Bethsaida

Capernaum

Gennesaret

GALILEE

SEA
OF
GALILEE

Nazareth

PALESTINE

RIVER JORDAN

Jerusalem

Bethany

0   10   20 miles

DEAD
SEA

Nazareth, where Jesus is commonly believed to have grown up, was a rather insignificant town – some argue that it did not even exist at that time. Capernaum, however, where he chose to base his ministry, was a thriving commercial centre. Jerusalem was the religious and political capital of Palestine. It is surrounded by hills, one of which is the Mount of Olives.

Most people lived in very basic houses built of mud or stone, often sharing their homes with their animals. The routines of life followed the seasons as many people were involved in agriculture. Most would have kept goats and sheep. The area was quite fertile, growing a range of fruit, grain and vegetables. Fish and bread were staples of their diet.

Jews of the time, as is still the case for many orthodox Jews today, followed very strict laws. The Old Testament tells the story of how these laws, the Torah, were handed down from God to Moses. Pharisees were teachers of the law who felt responsible for ensuring that people kept the laws. They were very concerned when Jesus seemed to challenge the Torah.

Finding out more

We recommend the following books and websites to gain a greater understanding of the New Testament.

Books

We strongly recommend that you read the rest of the *Real Reads* New Testament series, as the six narratives interlock to give a more complete picture of events. These are *Mary of Galilee, Simon Peter, Judas Iscariot, Mary Magdalene* and *Paul of Tarsus*.

* *New Century Youth Bible*, Authentic Lifestyle, 2007.

* Sally Lloyd-Jones, *The Jesus Storybook Bible: Every Story Whispers his Name*, Zondervan, 2007.

* J. R. Porter, *Jesus Christ: The Jesus of History, The Christ of Faith*, Duncan Baird, 1999. The photographs in this book offer a fascinating view of Palestine.

Websites

- www.bbc.co.uk/religion/religions/christianity
Lots of information about Jesus, history, and the Christian faith.

- www.localhistories.org/new.html
Brief but useful descriptions of many aspects of everyday life in New Testament times.

- www.rejesus.co.uk
Lots of interesting information about Jesus.

TV and film

- *Jesus of Nazareth*, directed by Franco Zeffirelli. ITV DVD, 1977. A six and a half hour mini-series.

- *The Miracle Maker*, directed by Derek Hayes and Stanislav Sokolov, ICON Home Entertainment, 2000. Animation.

- *The Parables of Jesus*, Boulevard Entertainment, 2006.

Food for thought

Here are some things to think about if you are reading *Jesus of Nazareth* alone, and ideas for discussion if you are reading it with friends.

Starting points

● Why do you think John was baptising people? What did baptism mean to Jesus? Why do you think Christians still use baptism today?

● How do you think Jesus feels when he realises that he is God's son? How would you feel if you were given so much power and responsibility? What would you do? What does Jesus decide to do?

● Why do you think Jesus chose fishermen as his first disciples? What qualities do *you* look for in a friend?

● Why do you think the disciples wanted to send the children away (see page 34)? Why did Jesus particularly want to see the children? What did Jesus think adults could learn from children?

● Why do you think Jesus accepted that he had to die?

- Find as many instances as possible of Jesus teaching people how to behave. Write a list of his 'instructions'. How might Christians today apply these instructions to their own lives?

- Christians believe that Jesus was and is both human and divine. Can you find any examples of Jesus struggling to be both?

- Why do you think the cross is an important symbol for Christians?

Group activities

- With a group of friends, take the roles of Jesus and the other characters from the book, and act one of the main scenes.

- Talk about what Jesus's friends thought about him, what his enemies thought, and what Jesus said about himself.

- Roleplay the different people on the day Jesus entered Jerusalem – the crowds, the disciples, Jesus. Afterwards, discuss the characters' feelings.

- In your group, imagine what would happen if Jesus returned today. This could be the beginning of all sorts of exciting and imaginative activities!